# URBAN LEGENDS · DON'T READ ALONE!

# BERMUDA TRIANGLE

This series features unsolved mysteries, urban legends, and other curious stories. Each creepy, shocking, or befuddling book focuses on what people believe and hear. True or not? That's for you to decide!

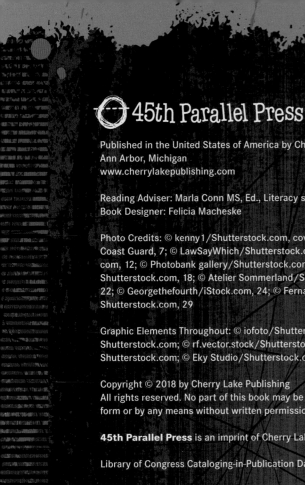

# 45th Parallel Press

Published in the United States of America by Cherry Lake Publishing
Ann Arbor, Michigan
www.cherrylakepublishing.com

Reading Adviser: Marla Conn MS, Ed., Literacy specialist, Read-Ability, Inc.
Book Designer: Felicia Macheske

Photo Credits: © kenny1/Shutterstock.com, cover; © Everett Historical/Shutterstock.com, 5; © United States Coast Guard, 7; © LawSayWhich/Shutterstock.com, 8; © Lightguard/iStock.com, 11; © JonMilnes/Shutterstock.com, 12; © Photobank gallery/Shutterstock.com, 15; © d13/Shutterstock.com, 17; © Marcin Niemiec/Shutterstock.com, 18; © Atelier Sommerland/Shutterstock.com, 21; © Michael Rosskothen/Shutterstock.com, 22; © Georgethefourth/iStock.com, 24; © Fernando Cortes/Shutterstock.com, 27; © Sergey Novikov/Shutterstock.com, 29

Graphic Elements Throughout: © iofoto/Shutterstock.com; © COLCU/Shutterstock.com; © spacedrone808/Shutterstock.com; © rf.vector.stock/Shutterstock.com; © donatas1205/Shutterstock.com; © cluckva/Shutterstock.com; © Eky Studio/Shutterstock.com

**45th Parallel Press** is an imprint of Cherry Lake Publishing.

Library of Congress Cataloging-in-Publication Data has been filed and is available at catalog.loc.gov

Cherry Lake Publishing would like to acknowledge the work of The Partnership for 21st Century Skills. Please visit *www.p21.org* for more information.

Printed in the United States of America
Corporate Graphics

# TABLE OF CONTENTS

# Chapter One

# THE MYSTERY OF FLIGHT 19

What happened to Flight 19? How is it connected to the Bermuda Triangle?

Something odd happened. It happened on December 5, 1945. Five Navy planes took off. They left from Fort Lauderdale, Florida. They flew over the Atlantic Ocean.

They were **training**. Training means practicing. They practiced flying. They practiced dropping bombs. The **mission** was called Flight 19. A mission is a job. It wasn't special. Training happens all the time.

Flight 19 was going well. Then, something went wrong. Their **compass** stopped working. A compass is a tool. It helps pilots find places.

The Flight 19 planes were torpedo bombers.

# CONSIDER THE EVIDENCE

Flight 19 made the Bermuda Triangle popular. But many disappearances happened before it. The USS *Cyclops* was a large ship. It weighed 19,000 tons. It carried materials. The materials were needed to make weapons. It had over 300 people on board. It crossed the Bermuda Triangle. It disappeared on March 4, 1918. Nothing was left behind. It made a record in U.S. naval history. It's the largest loss of life not caused by war. Some believe Germans took the ship. The Germans said they didn't. Some believe it had engine trouble. Some believe it sank in a storm. But no one really knows.

The planes flew the wrong way. There was rain. There were winds. There were clouds. One of the **airmen** said, "I don't know where we are. We must have got lost after that last turn." Airmen are pilots and crew members.

Fourteen airmen were on the planes. The planes and airmen **disappeared**. They were never seen again.

Another plane went after Flight 19. It had 13 airmen. It flew over the same area. It also disappeared. Navy experts studied what happened. They said this plane exploded. It blew up in the air. The plane was not safe. It was known to catch on fire.

The Navy sends out search-and-rescue teams.

The ocean is vast. It's mysterious.

Over 300 boats and planes looked for the lost planes. They looked for five days. They looked at over 300,000 square miles (776,996 square kilometers). The area was called the Bermuda Triangle. They didn't find anything. They didn't find bodies. They didn't find plane pieces.

Navy experts were stumped. They didn't know why Flight 19 disappeared. First, they blamed "pilot **error**." Error is a mistake. Later, they blamed "causes or reasons unknown."

The mystery of Flight 19 is unsolved. It inspired stories. It made the Bermuda Triangle famous. People wondered about the area. They thought it was dangerous.

# Chapter Two

# THE DEVIL'S TRIANGLE

Where is the Bermuda Triangle? How did it get its name? What is it like?

The Bermuda Triangle looks like a triangle. It's in the Atlantic Ocean. It's between Miami, Bermuda, and San Juan. Miami is in Florida. Bermuda is an island. San Juan is in Puerto Rico.

The Triangle is huge. It's about 500,000 square miles (1.3 million square km) of sea.

Vincent Gaddis was a reporter. He wrote for magazines. He wrote about this area. He did this in 1964. He came up with the name. He called it the "deadly Bermuda Triangle."

The Bermuda Triangle is larger than Texas, Louisiana, and Oklahoma combined.

Shipwrecks are preserved better in deeper water.

Many people, planes, and boats have gotten lost in this area. They've disappeared into thin air. They've disappeared underwater.

About 20 boats and 4 planes are lost every year. They disappear without a trace. There are no bodies. There's no **rubble**. Rubble is like trash. It's pieces from boats and planes. That's why it's also called the "Devil's Triangle." Some believe the devil lives there. They blame the devil.

# SPOTLIGHT BIOGRAPHY

Dr. Kenneth McAll is a psychiatrist. He's from England. He wrote a book. The title is *Healing the Haunted*. He took a cruise. He passed through the Bermuda Triangle. He wrote about his odd experiences. He heard "mournful singing." Mournful means sad. He thinks the singers were ghosts of African slaves. British sea captains sometimes drowned slaves. They threw people overboard. They did this on purpose. They tricked insurance companies. They claimed losses for extra money. He thinks the Bermuda Triangle is cursed. He thinks the area is haunted. He thinks the ghosts of those people are getting even.

The Bermuda Triangle has deep **trenches**. It has some of the world's deepest trenches. Trenches are long holes. They're narrow holes. They're on the seafloor. Bodies and rubble sink. They sink into these trenches. They are too deep to be reached.

The area has dangers. It has unsafe ridges. The ridges are sharp. They're made of rock or sand. The area has high waves. It has strong **currents**. Currents are water flows.

Weather is rough. There are many storms. There are many **hurricanes**. Hurricanes are storms with heavy winds.

Hurricanes can cause a lot of damage.

# Chapter Three

# THE CASE OF COLUMBUS'S COMPASS

How does the Bermuda Triangle affect compasses? How is Christopher Columbus connected to the Bermuda Triangle?

The Bermuda Triangle is special. It's different from other places. It affects compasses. This makes directions unstable.

It creates confusion. People lose their way. They don't know where they are. They don't know where they're going.

It's believed only two places do this. One is the Bermuda Triangle. The other is the Dragon's Triangle. This area is by Japan. It's off Japan's east coast. It's also known as the "Devil's Sea."

Explorers have to use many tools. They need to find their way.

Columbus described the light as "a small wax candle that rose and lifted up."

Christopher Columbus was an explorer. He explored the area. He did this in 1492. Strange things happened. He wrote about them. He wrote in his journals. This was the first record of this area.

His compass stopped working. He didn't tell his crew. He didn't want to worry them.

He also saw an odd light. The light was like a flame. He probably saw a **meteor**. A meteor is a space rock falling toward Earth. It leaves a trail of light.

# REAL-WORLD
# CONNECTION

Matt Smith is British. He's a reporter. His grandparents were on a plane. The plane was called *Star Tiger*. It disappeared in the Bermuda Triangle. This happened in 1948. There was a five-day search. Nothing was found. Smith said, "It's always been a mystery in my family. I grew up knowing that my grandparents weren't around. That they disappeared… We are trying to get to the mystery of how a plane could disappear and nothing found." He investigated. He made a documentary. A documentary is a nonfiction movie. It's called *Bermuda Triangle: The Missing Family*. Smith's mother was six months old when her parents died.

# Chapter Four

# TALES OF THE BERMUDA TRIANGLE

What are supernatural theories? How do some people explain the Bermuda Triangle?

Some people have **supernatural theories**. Supernatural means beyond science. Theories are ideas. They explain things.

Some believe in Atlantis. Atlantis was an island. It had a perfect city on it. The city had gold. It had silver. It had gems. But it disappeared.

Some believe Atlantis sank in the Bermuda Triangle. Energy crystals had powered the lost city. These crystals caused the disappearance. They cause the disappearances today.

Some thought they had proof of Atlantis. They looked at a nearby island. They saw walls and streets. Scientists found them to be just rocks.

Scientists doubt Atlantis existed.

Some blame **aliens**. Aliens are creatures. They're from outer space. Some think aliens live in this area. These aliens mess with our tools. That's why compass readings are odd.

Some blame **UFOs**. UFO means unidentified flying object. Aliens fly UFOs. That's how they come to Earth. They created a **base**. A base is a station. Their base is deep underwater. It's in the Bermuda Triangle. Aliens fly UFOs into the base.

Some people blame sea monsters.

# INVESTIGATION TIPS

- Interview someone who studies the Bermuda Triangle. Learn all the facts you can.

- Interview someone who's traveled in that area. Ask if they've had weird experiences.

- Learn about magnetic north. Learn about "true north." Understand navigation. Navigation is a science. It's how people find places. People plan paths based on positions.

- Practice using a compass. Learn how to read it.

- Practice using maps. Maps are great tools. (Don't rely solely on technology. Go old school!)

- Study travel patterns. Study paths to the Bermuda Triangle. Study paths from it.

Some people like time travel stories.

Some think the area is a special door. It opens up several times a year. It leads to another world. Lost people enter this world. They live different lives.

Some think the area is a time machine. It spins. It makes a time tunnel. It sends things off course. It does this quickly. Bruce Gernon is a pilot. He flew in this area. He thinks he traveled in time. He lost 28 minutes. His plane wasn't on any **radars**. Radars are special tools. They track planes' movements.

# Chapter Five

# TRIANGLE OF TRUTH, MAYBE?

## How do scientists explain the Bermuda Triangle?

Scientists have their own theories. Some believe the area makes gas. Gas gets trapped under the seafloor. The ocean farts it out. This forms underwater volcanoes. Volcanoes push out bubbles. Bubbles sink boats.

Some blame nature. Bad weather causes problems. Rain and wind can sink boats. Fog and storms can crash planes. Also, the sea is dangerous. It's huge. Huge waves can turn boats over.

Some blame humans. Humans make mistakes. Their mistakes can crash planes. Mistakes can sink boats. Some blame **pirates**. Pirates attack boats. They rob boats. They sink boats on purpose.

Some people like fiction more than facts.
They like the mystery of the Bermuda Triangle.

# EXPLAINED BY SCIENCE

What really happened to Flight 19? No one knows for sure. But some scientists have an idea. The fact is the planes got lost. They might have run out of gas. They weren't planning on flying that long. They didn't have enough gas. The planes crashed into the sea. The chance of surviving crashes is low. Some airmen could've survived the crash. But they wouldn't have lived much longer. Seas were rough. Weather was stormy. Waves were 50 feet (15 meters) high. Water was freezing cold. Any survivors would've froze to death.

Many scientists deny the Bermuda Triangle. They say it's not real. The Navy says it isn't real. The Coast Guard says it isn't real. It's not on any official maps.

The area is believed to be safe. People say the number of losses is normal. It's a major shipping lane. Many boats and planes travel it. It's not any more dangerous than other places. It's just more crowded.

The Gulf Stream is a current. It passes through the area. It washes things away. This explains why there's no evidence.

Real or not? It doesn't matter. The Bermuda Triangle lives in people's imaginations.

The Gulf Stream quickly washes things away.

# DID YOU KNOW?

- The Bermuda Triangle has several names. One name is "the Hoodoo Sea." Hoodoo means witchcraft. It also means bad luck.

- The Navy investigated Flight 19's disappearance. There was an official report. Someone noted that it was "as if they had flown to Mars." No one knew what happened.

- Dragon's Triangle is named after a Chinese myth. Myths are stories. Some people believed in dragons. Dragons lived deep underwater. Dragons moved. This created storms and fogs. Their movements sunk boats.

- The U.S. government created AUTEC. AUTEC stands for Atlantic Undersea Test and Evaluation Center. The Navy tests things there. It's in the Bermuda Triangle. Some people said they saw UFOs there.

- Some believe there's a monster called Bermuda Beast. It lives in the Bermuda Triangle. It's huge. It jumps out of water. It catches planes in midair. It eats them whole. It does the same to boats. It's based on a monster from Greek myths. It has a huge mouth.

- William Shakespeare wrote plays. He wrote a play called *The Tempest*. A tempest is a storm. His play is based on a ship in a storm. *The Sea Venture* was a 17th-century English ship. It was heading to Virginia. It fought a storm for three days. But it survived. All 150 people and one dog landed safely.

# CONSIDER THIS!

**Take a Position:** Consider why some scientists don't think the Bermuda Triangle exists. Do you think the Bermuda Triangle really exists or not? Argue your point with reasons and evidence.

**Say What?** The Bermuda Triangle fascinates people. Explain why the Bermuda Triangle is interesting. What makes it so mysterious?

**Think About It!** Would you be scared to travel in or near the Bermuda Triangle? Why or why not?

## LEARN MORE

- Bingham, Jane. *The Bermuda Triangle*. Chicago: Heinemann-Raintree, 2013.
- Omoth, Tyler. *Handbook to Stonehenge, the Bermuda Triangle, and Other Mysterious Locations*. North Mankato, MN: Capstone Press, 2017.
- Richard, Orlin. *The Bermuda Triangle*. North Mankato, MN: Child's World, 2015.

## GLOSSARY

**airmen** (AIR-muhn) pilot and crew members who work on a plane

**aliens** (AY-lee-uhnz) creatures from outer space

**base** (BASE) station, headquarters

**compass** (KUHM-puhs) a navigational tool that helps find positions and directions

**currents** (KUR-uhnts) flows of water

**disappeared** (dis-uh-PEERD) vanished, got lost, left without a trace

**error** (ER-ur) mistake

**hurricanes** (HUR-ih-kaynz) storms with heavy winds

**meteor** (MEE-tee-ur) a space rock falling toward Earth

**mission** (MISH-uhn) a quest, a job, a task

**pirates** (PYE-rits) robbers who attack and sink boats

**radars** (RAY-dahrz) special tools that track movements

**rubble** (RUHB-uhl) trash, wreckage pieces

**supernatural** (soo-pur-NACH-ur-uhl) things that can't be explained by science, like ghosts and aliens

**theories** (THEER-eez) ideas that explain something

**training** (TRAYN-ing) opportunities to practice skills

**trenches** (TRENCH-iz) long, narrow depressions or holes in the ground

**UFOs** (YOO-EF-OHZ) unidentified flying objects like spaceships

## INDEX

## ABOUT THE AUTHOR

Dr. Virginia Loh-Hagan is an author, university professor, former classroom teacher, and curriculum designer. She thinks her laundry room is the Bermuda Triangle; she's always losing clothes in there. She lives in San Diego with her very tall husband and very naughty dogs. To learn more about her, visit www.virginialoh.com.